Prayer 101
Going Back to the Basics

Lisa Marshall

DEDICATION

This book is dedicated to my sweet mother, Barbara Allen. One thing I am sure of is that my mom will pray when she gets up in the morning, before she goes to bed each night, before every meal, and all throughout the day. I've listened to that beautiful "sound" from her my entire life; it's priceless to me.

+++

CONTENTS

FOREWARD

A few years ago I taught a series on prayer at a local nursing home once a month for a six-month period. In preparing for these lessons, the task at hand was to simplify my current lessons on prayer. As I began to do this, I realized that in my endeavor to be profound and thought provoking, I had somewhat lost sight of the simple truths and concepts of prayer. In my quest to make it easy to understand for my audience at Delmar Gardens Nursing Home, I got a whole new education on the subject of prayer.

Too often I think we complicate things. Prayer really doesn't have to be complex. A friend of mine who is an elementary school teacher told me that when she really wants to understand a particular subject or event, she tries to find a children's book on the subject. The reason is because children's books usually take out all the "fluff," break it down, and make it easy and simple to understand.

In my fifteen years at World Network of Prayer I have found that many people are trying to build a strong prayer life but lack a foundation, just as a strong natural structure requires a solid foundation. In this book, I am going to try to assist you in building or solidifying the foundation for prayer in your life by going back to the basics of prayer.

Welcome to Prayer 101.

LISA MARSHALL

WHAT IS PRAYER?

It has been said that prayer is one of our greatest blessings and one of our biggest struggles. I would be inclined to agree.

Prayer defined is "to petition, beseech, to make a request, to ask, and an act of communion with God." Communion defined is "a close relationship with someone." So prayer could be defined as a "close relationship with God."

"Seriously?" you might ask. "Are you saying that prayer is not me getting on my knees and spending the entire time sharing with God every need I can think of, while telling Him the proper way to solve the issue?"

I'm afraid so.

Prayer is a close relationship with God in which we talk to Him and He talks to us. We are flesh and blood; God is a Spirit. Prayer bridges that gap between flesh and Spirit.

While they are very sincere in their beliefs, I do feel that many people have somewhat of a misconception about the exact nature of prayer. A friend contacted me recently and told me she had heard a song by Jaron Lowenstein about prayer and wanted me to hear it. I told her to send it to me and she did. Here are the lyrics:

> "I haven't been to church since I don't remember when
> Things were going great till they fell apart again
> So I listened to the preacher as he told me what to do
> He said, 'You can't go hating others
> who have done wrong to you'
> Sometimes we get angry, but we must not condemn
> Let the good Lord do His job; you just pray for them."

Sounds good so far, but the theme suddenly changes:

> "I pray your brakes go out runnin' down a hill
> I pray a flower pot falls from a window sill
> And knocks you in the head like I'd like to
> I pray your birthday comes and nobody calls
> I pray you're flyin' high and your engine stalls
> I pray all your dreams never come true
> Just know wherever you are, I pray for you."

You see, much like the person who wrote this song, there are a lot of misconceptions about prayer. Hopefully no one really has the view of prayer the author of this song has, but my guess is some do. Others feel prayer is a time for them to do all the talking and God all the listening. It is funny if you think about it. I can talk all day and nothing happens. God speaks and the universe is created. Yet why is it that when I have an audience with Him, I want to monopolize the conversation?

Before we can have a strong prayer life, it is imperative that we understand what prayer is. Prayer is "communication" with God. If I get down on my knees and spend an hour talking, have I communicated *with* God or have I talked *to* God? Make sure during your time of prayer that you get quiet and listen. It doesn't make much sense to ask God a lot of questions ("God, what should I do? . . . Where should I live? . . . Who should I marry?") and never stop to listen for the answer. Make silence a part of your prayer life. I think you will find you will accomplish a lot more. It is kind of silly that we start using filler trying to fill up an hour, when in fact we would make God very happy and make things much easier on ourselves if we spent part of our time "listening," reading His Word, and worshiping Him.

I have to confess, the most powerful times I've had in prayer have been when I said very little and let God do most of the talking.

WHY PRAY?

Why do you pray? Have you ever just stopped and asked yourself that question?

Why do you pray? Does God need help getting things done? Is He not able to do whatever He desires? Is He not self-sufficient?

If you ever want to be all you can be in Christ, you must answer that question in your own life and understand the biblical mandate of prayer. If you don't, prayer will always end up in a place of low priority in your life. And if it continues at the bottom of the list you will become ineffective and eventually carnal.

So why do you pray? Let's see what the Word has to say about it.

Why pray? The first reason, and quite possibly the most important, is because **Jesus told us to pray**

. . . and repeated the mandate several times.

"Continue earnestly in prayer, being vigilant in it with thanksgiving" (Colossians 4:2).

"Rejoice always, pray without ceasing, in everything give thanks; for this is the will of God in Christ Jesus for you" (I Thessalonians 5:16-18).

"Be anxious for nothing, but in everything by prayer and supplication, with thanksgiving, let your requests be made known unto God" (Philippians 4:6).

"Then He spoke a parable unto them, that men always ought to pray and not lose heart" (Luke 18:1).

"Offer to God thanksgiving, and pay your vows to the Most High. Call upon Me in the day of trouble; I will deliver you, and you shall glorify me" (Psalm 50:14-15).

Sounds to me as though it's pretty clear God wants us to pray. In both the Old and New Testaments, we find clear instructions that it was God's intention that we pray.

Why Pray? **Because it is expected.**

"And when you pray, you shall not be like the hypocrites. For they love to pray standing in the synagogues and on the corners of the streets, that they may be seen by men. Assuredly, I say to you, they have their reward. But you, when you pray, go into your room, and when you have shut your door, pray to your Father

who is in the secret place; and your Father who sees in secret will reward you openly. And when you pray*, do not use vain repetitions as the heathen do. For they think that they will be heard for their many words. Therefore do not be like them. For your Father knows the things you have need of before you ask Him. In this manner,* therefore, pray: *Our Father in heaven, Hallowed be Your name" (Matthew 6:5-9, emphasis mine).*

Now does it really sound as if prayer is optional? In these few short verses, God does not once say "if" you pray, but rather He says multiple times, "when" you pray.

When I was a teenager and my mom said, "Lisa, when you clean your room, I want you to change your sheets." That did not mean if I happened to get bored and have nothing to do, then it would be okay to clean my room. That meant more along the lines of "When I get home from work today, I fully expect to find your room neat and with clean sheets on the bed."

It seems rather clear to me that God expects us to pray.

Why pray? **Because it is encouraged with promises.**

I think God understood human nature and knew in order for us to be committed to something, we had to feel as though we were getting something out of it. The great thing about prayer is the many promises that come along with it.

> *"Now it came to pass, as He was praying in a certain place, when He ceased, that one of His disciples said to Him, 'Lord, teach us to pray, as John also taught his disciples.' So He said to them, 'When you pray, say: 'Our Father in heaven, hallowed be Your name. Your kingdom come. Your will be done on earth as it is in heaven. Give us day by day our daily bread. And forgive us our sins, for we also forgive everyone who is indebted to us. And do not lead us into temptation, but deliver us from the evil one.' And He said to them, 'Which of you shall have a friend, and go to him at midnight and say to him, "Friend, lend me three loaves; for a friend of mine has come to me on his journey, and I have nothing to set before him"'; and he will answer from within and say, "Do not trouble me; the door is now shut, and my children are with me in bed; I cannot rise and give to you'." I say to you, though he will not rise and give to him because he is his friend, yet because of his persistence he will rise and give him as many as he needs. So I say to you, ask, and it will be given to you; seek, and you will find; knock, and it will be opened to you. For everyone who asks receives, and he who seeks finds, and to him who knocks it will be opened"'* (Luke 11:1-10).

> *"Is anyone among you suffering? Let him pray. Is anyone cheerful? Let him sing psalms. Is anyone among you sick? Let him call for the elders of the church, and let them pray over him, anointing him with oil in the name of the Lord. And the prayer of faith will save the sick, and the Lord will raise him up. And if he has committed sins, he will be forgiven. Confess your trespasses to one another, and pray for one another, that you may be healed. The effective,*

fervent prayer of a righteous man avails much" (James 5:13-16).

Why pray? **Because it is needed.**

In Ephesians chapter six, the Bible tells us that we do not wrestle against flesh and blood, but against principalities, against powers, against the rulers of the darkness of this world, against spiritual wickedness in high places. It goes on to instruct us to take on the "whole armor of God" to withstand these invisible foes.

Let's say a person gets mad at me and decides to beat me up. I can see and hear them coming my way. At that point I have a choice: stay and try to defend myself or run in the opposite direction. Unfortunately, we don't have that option by default in the spirit world. Opposing spirits aren't flesh and blood; we can't see them coming at us. Prayer is needed to open our "spiritual eyes." Often when we pray, God will begin to reveal things to us. At times in my own personal life, God has shared with me specific things that were coming against me. This enabled me to pray strategically as well as guard myself with my armor.

Why pray? **Because it is effective and important.**

"Then another angel, having a golden censer, came and stood at the altar. He was given much incense, that he should offer it with the prayers of all the saints upon the

golden altar which was before the throne. And the smoke of the incense, with the prayers of the saints, ascended before God from the angel's hand" (Revelation 8:3-4).

Your prayers are so important that God saves every one of them.

Why pray? **So we may prosper in communion with God.**

"If ye abide in me, and my words abide in you, ye shall ask what ye will, and it shall be done unto you" (John 15:7).

"Seeing then that we have a great high priest, that is passed into the heavens, Jesus the Son of God, let us hold fast our profession. For we have not an high priest which cannot be touched with the feeling of our infirmities; but was in all points tempted like as we are, yet without sin. Let us therefore come boldly unto the throne of grace, that we may obtain mercy, and find grace to help in time of need" (Hebrews 4:14-16).

Prayer is the lifeline to the One I love most. Throughout His Word, He instructs us to pray, and by doing so we can reap our share of the benefits that result.

PRAYER IS IMPORTANT

Prayer is important.

- Prayer kept Joseph from getting bitter and from yielding to temptation.
- Prayer enabled David to slay a giant.
- Prayer helped Shadrach, Meshach, and Abednego to stand for God when everyone else was bowing down.
- Prayer is important for protection and spiritual growth of our children.

Samuel was able to hear the voice of God and say, "Here am I, Lord" because he had a mother named Hannah who knew how to pray.

I know without a doubt that I am here today because I had a mother who faithfully prayed for me.

A great example of the importance of prayer can be found in Luke chapter eleven. The disciples came to Jesus and said, "Lord, teach us to pray." This request was interesting because the disciples had been with Jesus for quite some time observing all the miraculous things He did: heal the sick, feed the thousands, raise the dead, calm storms, cast out demons, and open blind eyes. Why didn't they ask Him how to do all of these miraculous things that drew the crowds? Instead, they asked Him to teach them how to pray. My guess is they knew prayer was the most important thing. If they got that right, all the other things would be a byproduct of a strong prayer life.

I am not always a big fan of extremely modern translations of the Bible, although I did stumble upon one verse that I liked. James 5:16 says "the effectual fervent prayer of a righteous man availeth much." The modern translation renders the same verse, "When God's people pray, GREAT things happen!"

How important is prayer to you? It should be the most important thing in your life. If it is not, I strongly urge you to reprioritize.

DIFFERENT TYPES OF PRAYER

There are several different types of prayer. In this chapter we will discuss a few.

PETITION. This is when I pray for myself or for something I need.

INTERCESSION. This is when I pray for or on behalf of another person.

PRAYER OF FAITH. This is prayer rooted in our confidence in God's Word, knowing His will and praying and receiving it from Him.

PRAYER OF AGREEMENT. This is when two or more people agree with one another and with the Word of God that something specific will be done.

PRAISE AND THANKSGIVING. Giving thanks, glory, and honor to God for what He has done.

BINDING AND LOOSING. Taking authority over spirits. Whatever we as Christians do in His name here on earth, it will be carried through by the Father in Heaven.

REPENTANCE. Confessing our faults to our Father who will forgive us.

PRAYING THE WORD. Using portions of the Word of God as our prayers.

DIFFERENT POSITIONS OF PRAYER

There are many different positions of prayer mentioned in the Bible. When Jesus prayed, He looked up to Heaven. Moses lifted his hands. Abraham's servant bowed his head and worshiped the Lord. King Solomon stood before the altar and spread his hands toward Heaven. Elijah "cast himself down upon the earth, and put his face between his knees." Elisha paced back and forth. Communication with God doesn't require a particular physical position of prayer. However, the posture we use often gives the expression of the attitude of our hearts. Let's look at a few.

Sitting denotes rest (I Chronicles 17:16; Acts 2:1-2).

Kneeling denotes surrender. Shows a sign of personal humility (I Kings 8:54; Ezra 9:5; Luke 22:41; Acts 9:40).

Bowing displays honor and humility. Shows

reverence (Exodus 34:8; Psalm 72:11; Nehemiah 8:6).

Standing is a position of respect and honor. Shows readiness to receive instructions (Nehemiah 9:5; Mark 11:25).

Uplifted hands acknowledges a place of surrender. No weapons; no hidden agenda; a position of praise (II Chronicles 6:12; I Timothy 2:8; I Kings 8:54; Nehemiah 8:6).

Walking denotes a warring position. It stirs up your prayer intensity (II Kings 4:33-35).

Prostrating shows awe of the holiness of God. A position of humility; a position of repentance (Joshua 7:6; Ezra 10:1; Matthew 26:39; Mark 14:35).

As you can see there are many ways we can pray. I believe God is more interested in the position of our heart than the position of our body. I personally like different positions of prayer depending on how I am praying. When I am enjoying a deep time with God, I tend to pray bowing or lying prostrate. When I feel worshipful, I raise my hands. When I am warring in the spirit, I usually walk. Well, to be honest, I probably stomp more than walk. The more intense the prayer time gets, the faster I pace back and forth. When I am enjoying communion with God, I will kneel or even sit.

Someone told me that when they pray early in the morning they often struggle with getting sleepy, so they practice all the prayer positions during their time of prayer. It helps keep them alert and varies their prayer activities.

I say do whatever works for you. For some who have health issues or are advanced in age, bowing or lying prostrate is quite difficult. For them, sitting would be much easier. Keep in mind, the greatest prayer meeting of all time took place in an upper room where they were "sitting." Find what works for you. The important thing is not what position you use, but rather that you pray.

HINDRANCES TO PRAYER

I remember it well. I had just spent what seemed like hours praying. It was probably more like five minutes, but for a kid my age, that was a long time. As I got up weary from my time of intercession, my granny looked at me and asked in a way that only Gran could, "Do you think your prayers made it to the ceiling?"

Well Gran, I cannot begin to tell you how many times since that day I have wondered the same thing. Has anyone besides me ever felt like your prayers weren't going anywhere? You pray and pray and nothing happens. You remind God that you belong to Him and the Bible says to "Ask and ye shall receive" (As if He didn't already know) still, nothing. What do you do?

What if your car wouldn't start? You turned the

key and nothing happened. Do you keep doing this for days or do you try to find the problem? You can turn the key all day every day, but if there is a mechanical problem, you will be sitting in the same place a year later getting the same result. Would it not make sense to have a mechanic look at it and find what is wrong?

Keep in mind God's timing isn't always our timing. Actually, I have found God's time is very seldom my timing, but He's God and He's good at it, so I will trust Him. There are times it "isn't time" and there are times it "isn't working". If it "isn't working", here are a few things that may be hindering your prayers.

Not fellowshipping with God. Fellowship means to have a partnership, or to spend time with. Why would God answer the prayers of someone who never speaks to Him?

Let's look at this in the natural and see if it makes sense to you. Let's pretend that I come up to you in church and pledge my loyalty and devotion to you. I vow to serve you and do anything you want me to do. Then we leave and I go home with you. As soon as we walk through the door of your home, I stop talking to you. I ignore you all week and don't say one word. Then on Wednesday, we go back to church and as soon as we walk through the doors of the church, I immediately begin telling you how important you are to me and how much I love you. I promise that I will do anything you ask...I even do so in tears. Then we go home and once again, I don't speak to you all for the next few days. You try to talk to me, but I am busy and ignore you. I might even make empty promises that I will make time for you later...but never do. We go back to church and suddenly you have my undivided attention. I weep. I cry. I vow to go to the far corners of the earth for you. I tell you non-stop how wonderful you are and sing your praises for all to hear. And then we leave.

Now be truthful...how many of you would put up with a friend that treated you that way? I personally don't really want people in my life like that. Do you? Yet, how many times, have we done that exact thing to God?

Not praying in Jesus' Name. Jesus instructed His disciples on how to pray. He said to pray in the name of Jesus. For it is THAT name that has all power. It is THAT name that makes demons tremble. It is THAT name that we can run into and find safety.

Not asking or asking with the wrong motives. Now if you don't ask, your prayer won't be answered for sure. Pretty deep, huh? Ye ask, and receive not, because ye ask amiss (or wrong). This tells me that God doesn't want us to pray selfishly. He wants more than your grocery list. Make prayer about God, not just about what you want or need.

Not asking according to God's will. The Bible tells us that if ask according to His will, he will hear us. (1 John 5:14-15) The great thing is His Will can be found by reading His Word. God will not answer a prayer that is against His will. *"God, let Sally fail math class"* or *"God, would you smite that person that just cut me off in traffic."* Now praying that may make you feel better at the moment, but God will never respond to those types of prayers. Search His Word for things he says is His will and pray them into being.

Not having God's Word in you. John 15:7 tells us "If you abide in Me and My words abide in you, ask what you desire and it shall be done for you." Makes it pretty clear that God expects us to read the Bible. When I don't know what to pray, I can always pray the Word of God. His Word is forever settled. Hide his Word in your heart.

Doubt & Unbelief. James 1:5-8 tells you to ask God in faith without doubting for your request to be fulfilled. Think back on a time God has answered a prayer for you or for someone you know. Think on the stories in the Bible where miracles took place. He is the same yesterday, today and forever. If He did it then, He can do it now! Pray and ask God believing that He will hear and answer your prayers.

Giving Up. Luke 18:1 tells us to pray and not to faint. In my personal life, I have often found that I feel the most like giving up right before my miracle happens. Jesus taught this "I'm not giving up prayer" in Luke 11 with the friend who needed bread and in Luke 18 with the widow and the unjust judge. No matter how long you have been praying, no matter how impossible the situation seems, don't give up!

Not being in agreement. Matthew 18:9 tells us "if any two of you agree, it will be done." It never ceases to amaze me that people go to a prayer meeting and yet everyone gets in their corner and prays for their own list of things. Not sure how much agreement is going on. Whenever I have something in my life that is major and needs prayer, I go to a few people that I trust and ask them to agree with me. When we pray together in agreement, we become more powerful.

Unforgiveness. For if you forgive men their trespasses, your father will forgive yours. There are many people who can't seem to get their prayers answered and become frustrated. What they don't realize is the thing hindering them is unforgiveness toward someone. I must confess I have struggled with this one. It is difficult to understand why God expects us to forgive people who have done serious damage to us. I'm not talking about someone who spoke harshly to you. I'm talking about someone who really did you wrong and it left scars. Don't know why He requires it, but He does. We must forgive. Not matter how hard. No matter what the offense. The sad truth is a lot of good people are allowing a lot of bad people to keep them from getting their prayers answered.

Unconfessed Sin. Psalm 66:18 says "If I regard iniquity in my heart, the Lord will not hear me:" Basically God is saying, if there is sin there, I'm not going to hear your prayer. You may have all your friends fooled. You may have your family and fellow church members fooled…but God knows your heart and you will never fool Him

Now that this is out of the way, try the key again.

WHAT YOUR PRAYERS CAN DO FOR OTHERS

Prayer is a powerful thing. Not only does prayer affect the person praying, it can also have a profound impact on others. The Bible gives many examples of the results of prayer on the lives of others.

Your prayers can help protect others from temptation.

> *"And the Lord said, Simon, Simon, behold, Satan hath desired to have you, that he may sift you as wheat: but I have prayed for thee, that thy faith fail not: and when thou art converted, strengthen thy brethren" (Luke 22:31-32).*

Your prayers can contribute to the spiritual growth of others.

> *"Cease not to give thanks for you, making mention of you*

in my prayers; that the God of our Lord Jesus Christ, the Father of glory, may give unto you the spirit of wisdom and revelation in the knowledge of him: the eyes of your understanding being enlightened; that ye may know what is the hope of his calling, and what the riches of the glory of his inheritance in the saints" (Ephesians 1:16-18).

Your prayers can contribute to a peaceful society.

"I exhort therefore, that, first of all, supplications, prayers, intercessions, and giving of thanks, be made for all men; for kings, and for all that are in authority; that we may lead a quiet and peaceable life in all godliness and honesty" (I Timothy 2:1-2).

Your prayers can save someone's life.

"Now about that time Herod the king stretched forth his hands to vex certain of the church. And he killed James the brother of John with the sword. And because he saw it pleased the Jews, he proceeded further to take Peter also. (Then were the days of unleavened bread.) And when he had apprehended him, he put him in prison, and delivered him to four quaternions of soldiers to keep him; intending after Easter to bring him forth to the people. Peter therefore was kept in prison: but prayer was made without ceasing of the church unto God for him" (Acts 12:1-5).

"And, behold, the angel of the Lord came upon him, and a light shined in the prison: and he smote Peter on the side, and raised him up, saying, Arise up quickly. And his chains fell off from his hands. And the angel said unto

him, Gird thyself, and bind on thy sandals. And so he did. And he saith unto him, Cast thy garment about thee, and follow me" (Acts 12:7-8).

"And when Peter was come to himself, he said, Now I know of a surety, that the Lord hath sent his angel, and hath delivered me out of the hand of Herod, and from all the expectation of the people of the Jews" (Acts 12:11).

Your prayers can help others understand spiritual things.

"Cease not to give thanks for you, making mention of you in my prayers; that the God of our Lord Jesus Christ, the Father of glory, may give unto you the spirit of wisdom and revelation in the knowledge of him: the eyes of your understanding being enlightened; that ye may know what is the hope of his calling, and what the riches of the glory of his inheritance in the saints" (Ephesians 1:16-18).

Your prayers can move God to help someone.

"Confess your faults one to another, and pray one for another, that ye may be healed. The effectual fervent prayer of a righteous man availeth much" (James 5:16).

Your prayers can help pastors be successful in ministry.

"Now the God of hope fill you with all joy and peace in believing, that ye may abound in hope, through the power of the Holy Ghost" (Romans 15:13).

PRAY WITHOUT CEASING

"And he [Jesus] spake a parable unto them to this end, that men ought always to pray, and not to faint" (Luke 18:1).

"Pray without ceasing" (I Thessalonians 5:17).

The Bible tell us that we ought always to pray and to pray without ceasing. How exactly are we supposed to do this? Do we quit our jobs? Do we never sleep again? Of course neither of those ideas is a viable option. To pray without ceasing refers to recurring prayer, not non-stop talking.

A literal translation of the verse is to pray incessantly. Incessantly defined means 'continuing or occurring so frequently it almost seems uninterrupted.' A good example would be when you get a song stuck in your head and at various times throughout the day, before you even realize what you are doing, you are humming or singing the tune. Praying without ceasing simply means to be in a prayerful state of mind wherever you are, whatever you are doing.

A great way to accomplish this is to look for opportunities to pray. May I offer a few suggestions?

Sitting at a traffic light. Pray for the people in the cars around you. Pray for the area that you are in. Pray specifically for things around you that indicate a prayer need, or give thanks to God for the blessings you see.

Standing in line. Pray blessings on the business and all the employees that work there. Pray that each person that frequents the business will have a personal relationship with Christ.

While driving. Pray for the neighborhood. Pray for godliness and morality to prevail. If there are high crime areas, pray against strongholds. If the area is getting run-down, pray blessings of prosperity on the area.

On the job. Pray for God to open doors for you to be a witness and to share the gospel with your coworkers.

When cleaning or repairing the house. Cover each room and those who frequent them with prayer and protection. Assign prayer points to the different jobs you do.

School zone. With all the school shootings in

the past few years, our schools need prayer more than ever. While going through a school zone, pray for the teachers and the children. Pray for protection and safety.

Hospital or ambulance. The next time you pass a hospital or you see an ambulance, take a moment to pray for the sick and injured.

Pray blessings on the local economy, school boards, businesses, and other churches that are still in need of the revelation of Jesus.

Drug addict or billboard promoting alcohol. Pray down spiritual strongholds such as drug addiction, pornography, alcoholism, abuse, immorality, and nicotine.

A SIMPLE APPROACH TO THE LORD'S PRAYER

Have you ever been speechless?

I think we've all had those times when we just didn't know what to say. When the highway patrol officer asks you if you knew how fast you were driving. When you take that special someone on a date and the waitress brings you credit card back and tells you that it was declined. When you are trying to sneak back in after curfew and run into one of your parents in the hall.

We've all been there.

Have you ever got down to pray and the words just weren't there? Maybe because you've just been in God's presence to the point you are overwhelmed. Maybe because you have problems and your heart is so heavy with grief you just can't put it into words. Maybe it is because you have sin in your life and you are ashamed. For whatever the reason, I think Jesus understood that we would have those times. He knew that there would be times it would be difficult talking to Him unless we knew what to say so He gave us a sample prayer to help us.

"After this manner therefore pray ye: Our Father which art in heaven, Hallowed be thy name. Thy kingdom come, Thy will be done in earth, as it is in heaven. Give us this day our daily bread. And forgive us our debts, as we forgive our debtors. And lead us not into temptation, but deliver us from evil: For thine is the kingdom, and the power, and the glory, forever. Amen." (Matthew 6:9-13)

We know this as the Lord's Prayer. You can find it on plaques, bookmarks, and Bible covers. Most children can quote it.

Today we are going to take a look at the components of the Lord's Prayer. When you break down the King James English, this pattern that Jesus told us to follow really is quite simple.

OUR FATHER

It is always good to start off your prayer reminding yourself of your personal relationship to

God. He is your heavenly father, and He loves you because you are His child. To break it down even further…He is your daddy and you are his little boy or girl and He loves you very much.

WHICH ART IN HEAVEN

Praise God for His majesty. He is in control of the universe and nothing is too difficult for Him. He made all the planets, the stars, the trees and all the little animals. He created everything and He is watching over you daily.

HALLOWED BE THY NAME

This refers to the nature of God. He is worthy of respect and devotion. Our praise to Him is appropriate because of who He is. Praise Him for who He is to you.

JEHOVAH-TSIDKENU "our righteousness"

JEHOVAH-M'KADDESH "who sanctifies"

JEHOVAH-SHALOM "our peace"

JEHOVAH-SHAMMAH "Jehovah is there"

JEHOVAH-ROPHE "our healer"

JEHOVAH-JIREH "our provider"

JEHOVAH-NISSI "my banner"

JEHOVAH-ROHI "my shepherd"

What else is He to you? Friend. Confidant. Savior. Encourager.

THY KINGDOM COME

Pray that God's Kingdom will grow and flourish and what He wants will be accomplished.

THY WILL BE DONE ON EARTH AS IT IS IN HEAVEN

Ask God to be the primary influence in your life and for His priorities to be your priorities. Ask Him to help you crucify your own will

Pray God let Your will be done in…

- My life
- My ministry
- My family (spouse, children, other family members)
- My Church
- My Career

GIVE US THIS DAY OUR DAILY BREAD

Ask God for the things you need and be specific. Believe it is God's will to prosper you and that He wants to give you the things you need.

AND FORGIVE US OUR SINS

Take a moment and repent. Ask God to reveal anything in your life that displeases Him.

AS WE FORGIVE THOSE WHO SIN AGAINST US

Ask God to show you anyone you need to forgive.

AND LEAD US NOT INTO TEMPTATION, BUT DELIVER US FROM EVIL

Ask God to help you with any sin you are struggling with. Ask Him to make you strong when temptation comes your way. Be specific about your struggles. Be wise in not intentionally placing yourself in a position to be tempted.

Pray a hedge of protection around yourself. God, You are my refuge, my fortress, my God. Your Name is a strong tower I can run into and find safety.

Put on the whole armor of God

1. Helmet of SALVATION – protect my mind

2. Breastplate of RIGHTEOUSNESS – protect and keep my heart right

3. Loins girt about with TRUTH – let truth keep me from the lies of the enemy

4. Feet shod with the PREPARATION (readiness) of the gospel of PEACE – Guide my steps – let everywhere I walk bring peace

5. Shield of FAITH – quench the fiery darts of the enemy – help me believe when I don't understand

6. Sword of the Spirit (the Word of God) – let me be on the offensive with YOUR WORD for it is quick and powerful

FOR THINE IS THE KINGDOM, AND THE POWER, AND THE GLORY FOREVER AMEN

Make your faith declarations and end your time of prayer in praise to your powerful God.

KINGDOM PRAYING

"But seek ye first the kingdom of God, and his righteousness; and all these things shall be added unto you" (Matthew 6:33).

Have you ever analyzed your prayers? Are they more selfish or more selfless? If we are completely honest, most of us would have to confess our prayers are more selfish. We are like the young lady who prayed, "Lord, I ask nothing for myself, but please send my mother a handsome son-in-law."

More often than not, the prayers of the typical believer are self-focused. "God, bless me, my family, my health, my finances," and so on. Certainly God can and does bless us in all these areas and more, but when this is the exclusive focus of our prayers, it reflects that we have lost some valuable principles of prayer.

If every prayer you prayed in the last twenty-four hours was answered, would the Kingdom even know it? Sadly, for many, the answer would be no. My guess is a lot of people would be healed, financial problems would go away, and we would all like our jobs. But what impact on the Kingdom would there be?

Kingdom praying is praying for the things that will matter for eternity, not just our own personal needs. It is praying unselfishly about the things that are important to God. Kingdom-focused prayers end not in our own success and happiness, but in the building of God's kingdom and the power of His righteousness in the lives of His children.

In the Sermon on the Mount, Christ Jesus taught His disciples to pray "your kingdom come" and to "seek first the kingdom." In modern terms Jesus was saying if you will take care of My stuff first, then I will take care of yours.

We've got to learn to pray bigger than ourselves. We serve a big God, yet we pray such small prayers. If I hit my thumb with a hammer and hurt myself, I can spend my time praying for the pain to stop. If it does, my prayers have impacted one person. But if I pray for an open door for the gospel to go into China, my prayers have the potential of impacting 1.4 billion souls. Is it getting clearer to you? If you pray for China and India alone, you are praying for one out of every three people on this earth.

What we tend to do is spend the majority of our prayer time praying for our sore thumb and Sister Susie when half of the world has never even heard of Jesus. We must start praying bigger prayers.

The next time you pray for someone you know who has cancer, why not pray for all people who have cancer? Better yet, why not pray for a cure for cancer to be found? Instead of praying for your local church, pray for the global church and revival worldwide. Instead of praying just for your personal finances, pray for the finances needed to spread the gospel all over the world.

I think we have it backwards. We spend all of our prayer time praying for our needs, while neglecting the things of the Kingdom that will matter for eternity. We live in a society that feeds our ego. Burger King tells us to "have it your way" and McDonald's tells us we "deserve a break today." Magazines advise women they should take plenty of "me" time, lose weight, look beautiful, and be assertive. Ads persuade people to spend money on luxuries for themselves. It's no wonder we have become selfish in our prayers. Think beyond yourself and all of the "mys": my family, my church, my district, my friends, and so on.

There is nothing wrong with praying for those things; just don't make your prayer time all about you. Pray bigger next time. Seek first the Kingdom and watch God keep His Word and "add all these things.".

WHAT PRAYER IS NOT

While the majority of this book has been spent talking about what prayer is and more effective ways to do it, this chapter is dedicated to talking about what prayer is not.

Prayer is not leftovers you give to God. God wants to hear from us first while the day is fresh and new, before busyness and problems clutter the day. Prayer should never be our 'Plan B.' Many use prayer as a safety net. We try to fix a problem our way and then if it doesn't work, we go to Plan B—prayer—usually in crisis mode. If we would learn to pray first, we would be led by the Spirit and have peace in our life. We would not be stuck in a crisis trying to find God's will.

Prayer is not ever unanswered. God most often answers no, yes, or wait. Sometimes "no answer" is the answer. The key is to trust Him. No matter what the answer, He knows what is best. Sometimes God chastens us mildly by ignoring our prayers and severely by answering them!

Prayer is not a bargaining tool with God. "God, I will pray every day if you will do this for me . . ." I've found I shouldn't pray just when I have a need. I should pray because I love Him and because He is worthy. Ever have a friend that the only time you hear from them is when they want something? Nobody wants that kind of friend, including God.

Prayer is not God being your sugar daddy. Prayer should not be solely self-serving. Prayer should be about the Kingdom, not just so you can get something.

Prayer is not just bended knees. Prayer is a way of life. It is a constant state of mind. A place where we live.

Prayer is not ordinary. Prayer should be expecting the miraculous. It is an encounter with Almighty God. Prayer by its very nature is anything but ordinary.

Prayer is not solving issues for the Lord. Too often in prayer we spend the majority of our time telling God how to solve all the needs we bring before Him. I once heard someone say, "He is God and He's good at it, so let Him be God." Your job is to bring the need to God; His job is to come up with the solution. I have found that I don't always understand God's ways, and, more often than not, He doesn't do things in the way I thought He should. But I must trust Him to do what He knows is best.

Prayer is not a one-way conversation. Take time to listen to His voice. Read His Word and listen with an open heart. The greatest thing you can do during your prayer time is to be quiet.

Prayer is not a clocked event. It is relationship. It is spending time in His presence until you feel the release to leave.

Prayer is not idle words to fill time. It is not talking eloquently in order to impress someone. Just because we use the King James Version of the Bible doesn't mean we have to pray in King James English. He is our daddy. We can talk to Him as we would talk to our earthly father.

Prayer is not an option. It is not just a "good idea"; it is a biblical mandate and our lifeline to the Creator. If you are a Christian, you must pray.

Prayer is not magic. We cannot summon God as if He were a genie waiting to grant our wishes.

Prayer is not a means by which to escape the biblical principle of sowing and reaping. You will reap what you sow, no matter how much you try to pray your way out of it. If you take a gun and intentionally shoot someone, you can pray all day long, but you are still going to jail.

Prayer is not a guarantee against suffering. I have known many wonderful, godly Christians who have suffered and even some who have lost their lives. It seems so unfair. Yet the fact remains: it rains on the just and the unjust. Prayer won't keep you from suffering, but it will assuredly take you through it.

Prayer is not something we just do at church. Prayer should take place in our home much more so than at church. It is the place we spend the most time and should be a place of prayer. Jesus said His house would be called a house of prayer . . . our house should too.

A SEASON, A TIME, AND A WORD
The Progression of Prayer

Season - an indefinite period of time

Time – a measured or measurable period

Word - a brief remark or conversation

Would it ever end? I was certain I felt myself aging. There I was, waiting for it to be over and waiting for the Lord to return - wondering which would happen first.

The place? Prayer meeting!

I was seven. At that time, prayer was probably around number 208 on my list of priorities. I mean, after all God already knew our needs. He also already knew the future. So in my highly educated and intelligent seven-year-old mind, no matter how hard I tried, I just couldn't understand. If God knew what we needed and knew what we were going to ask for when we prayed, then locking ourselves in the church for what seemed to be an endless period of time to tell God what He already knew, seemed to me like a great big waste of time.

You see, during those days 36 years ago, the saints met frequently for what they called a "season" of prayer. In the little church where I grew up in Green Pond, Alabama, they were serious about it. They met with the intent and purpose to pray until something happened. If it took 30 minutes, fine. If it took five hours, that was fine too.

Jump forward a few years and more and more you began to hear the phrase "a time of prayer." Oh yes, make no mistake, there was still prayer meeting – it just didn't last quite as long. No more meeting to pray until you hear from heaven, now we were more on a time schedule. Okay God, you have from 7:00 – 8:00 PM on Monday night to show up, or we'll have to catch you next week. A "season" had somehow evolved to "a time."

Jump forward a few more years to our fast paced, push-button society where we've become accustomed to getting everything in a hurry. No more taking days or weeks to travel across country by horse or train admiring the beauty of the landscape that God created. Now we get on a plane and in two hours or less we can get 1,000 miles in any direction. No more taking hours to thaw something. Just pop it in the microwave and the same result is accomplished in mere minutes.

Wouldn't you know it? The church has also progressed. How many times in your local service or at larger events do we pause now to have a "word" of prayer?

How interesting. We have gone from a season, to a time, to a word. To borrow wisdom from Webster's dictionary, it would seem we have gone from "an indefinite period of prayer, to a measured or measurable period of prayer, to a brief remark or conversation with God."

It would almost seem that with all of our computers, gadgets and modern-day conveniences to help us save time, we have gotten so busy that we have almost phased prayer out completely. Makes me wonder about scriptures like:

1 Thessalonians 5:17, the Apostle Paul tells believers to "pray without ceasing."

Luke 21:36 – "Watch ye therefore, and pray always, that ye may be accounted worthy to escape all these things that shall come to pass, and to stand before the son of man."

While I know that we can't pray non-stop due to work schedules and the need for sleep, but speaking for myself, I could definitely dedicate more time to prayer. There are times when all we have time to do is utter a "word" of prayer. Other times our schedule may be a little more flexible, allowing us to devote a little "time" to prayer. But let us not forget that periodically, we must not neglect having a "season" of prayer. No matter how busy, periodically we must give ourselves to an extended period of seeking God. We need that – He does too!

I was at a church last week and someone told the congregation to just "breathe a prayer."

I wonder what will be next. God help us!

10 WAYS PRAYER IS LIKE RIDING A BICYCLE

1. **Anyone can do it**. You don't have to possess any particular qualities in order to pray. There is no magic button. We all get the same Holy Ghost. If He called you, you are equipped.

2. **You don't have to understand the mechanics to make it work.** Most people cannot produce the equations of how wheel velocity or angular momentum or electric current works. I can't explain how some things work either; I just know, for instance, when I hop on a bike and start pedaling, I'm off down the street. When I flip a light switch, I'm no longer in the dark. By the same token, you don't have to have a scientific brain in order to pray. Whether or not you understand how it works, it still works.

3. **Getting started is the hardest part.** When a child learns how to ride a bike, there is usually

an adult or older kid there to give them a push. It's very difficult for them to start from a dead stop. The same is true for prayer. You have to apply some self-discipline, especially at first. After a few weeks, it is easier to keep going because you have gained momentum.

4. **Balance is the key.** It is just as difficult to ride a bike without balance as it is to have a prayer life without balance. Give equal time to seeking His hands, His face, and His heart.
   - Hands – asking for His help.
   - Face – seeking His direction.
   - Heart – what does He love? What does He hate? Instead of asking God to anoint what you are doing, ask Him to direct you to the thing He can anoint.

5. **It helps to keep the tires full of air.** It is very difficult to ride a bike when the tires are flat. It is even difficult to push it. Air is the Holy Spirit in our lives, the breath of God. We need to be full of the Holy Spirit so He can guide and direct our prayers. There will be times we don't know what to pray. The Spirit will lead during these times.

6. **It makes sense to protect your head.** It is unwise to ride a bike without a helmet. Helmets protect bike riders from serious injury. In the same way, you need a "helmet" to guard against bad influences that can corrupt your mind: profane conversations, media intake, what you read, what you watch,

chats, texts, and so on. Each day, put on the helmet of salvation and ask God to protect your mind and thoughts.

7. **Some of the best trips are those without destinations in mind.** It is much more fun to joyride than to be sent on an errand. Prayer should be enjoyed, not an obligation you have to meet. Spend time in God's presence. Don't always be in a hurry. Lingering in His presence gives you a taste of "pleasures for evermore" (Psalm 16:11).

8. **The will be some hills.** Bike riders won't always be able to coast downhill; there are two sides to every hill, and one of them is up! Some days praying is like riding a bike to the top of a hill. You will labor in prayer for everyone and everything you know several times over and wear yourself out getting nowhere. Other days, you will coast right into God's presence and never want to leave.

9. **Brakes are as important as the pedals.** It is dangerous to ride a bike with no brakes; you will likely end up getting hurt. Likewise, prayer is not measured by how fast you go nonstop. At times it seems you could talk to God endlessly, but eventually you'll have to apply the brakes and just listen to see what He has to say. If you listen, you'll end up accomplishing a whole lot more than if you're the only one who's talking.

10. **You have to get up when you fall if you want to learn to ride.** No one learns to ride without falling at least once. If you quit after you fall, you will

never enjoy the pleasure of riding your bike. You may not get everything just right the first time you pray, but continue on. You will develop a deep, strong prayer life if you just get up and keep going.

PRACTICAL TIPS FOR PRAYER

Many people who visit the World Network of Prayer will ask, "What do you have that can help me pray better?" Others stop to share how they struggle with maintaining their daily prayer life. Some are even honest enough to share that they don't really have a prayer life and request material on how to start one.

The truth is, there is no secret formula or program for a life dedicated to prayer. It basically comes down to a person making the decision to have a consistent prayer life and then having the discipline to see it through.

Here are a few practical suggestions to get you started.

1. **Don't just talk about prayer, pray!** You can know everything there is to know about prayer, but if you don't pray, you are not affecting the Kingdom. Don't wait until the

mood hits or the perfect time materializes. The "perfect time" is now! Start now and make prayer a daily priority.

2. **Schedule a prayer time.** Setting aside time for prayer is the most important place to begin in developing your prayer life. If you never take time to pray, your prayer life will never grow and develop. Make an appointment with God, just as you schedule appointments with your doctor. Make note of it on your calendar. If it is not on your schedule, you are more likely to put it off. Make it a priority. If you can pray at the same time each day, you will find it easier to be consistent. It only takes twenty-one days to establish a habit. Many find it easier to pray first thing in the morning; some like to pray in the evening. Do what works for you. Although I do recommend that you never go into your day without pausing to ask God to guide your day and to pray on the armor of God.

3. **Create an environment for prayer.** Choose a quiet place. Prepare your surroundings by gathering inspirational material, worshipful music, a Bible, a list of missionaries, a globe, and a prayer journal. I also recommend you keep a notepad handy. As you pray things will come to mind. If you jot them down you won't forget and can return your focus to prayer. Also, God may give you a thought that you don't want to

forget.

4. **Prepare your heart and mind.** Start your prayer time asking God for insight and understanding as to what to pray for. Ask God to increase your faith. The Bible says "ask believing" and it shall be done.

5. **Pace yourself.** If you currently don't have an established prayer life, don't start with a goal to pray three hours a day. It is unlikely you will succeed. Instead, start with fifteen minutes a day. I have learned that the longer I pray, the longer I pray. Being interpreted, the longer (days, weeks, years) I pray, the longer (seconds, minutes, hours) I pray. When I first started I had to pray at least three times for everything I could think of to fill an hour. Now, many years down the road, I often find an hour is not enough time. If your goal is to pray an hour, start with fifteen minutes. Each week add another five minutes to your prayer time. You will reach the hour before you know it.

6. **Use a prayer wheel.** WNOP has a wonderful prayer wheel guide. It has twelve sections: praise, Kingdom praying forgiveness and confession, petition, intercession, Bible reading, meditation, thanksgiving, praying the Word, singing, listening, and praise. It is an excellent tool in helping to establish a consistent prayer life. The goal is to pray through each section. I

recommend you start with one minute in each section. The next week double it to two minutes per section and so on. In just five short weeks, you will be praying one hour per day using this guide. Since Barna reports that the average Christian spends less than six minutes per day praying, you will be way above the average.

7. **Be specific.** How many times do we pray, "God bless Brother John and Sister Sue"? Well, if someone walks up and gives Brother John a candy bar and gives Sister Sue a quarter, they have been blessed and our prayers have been answered. Wouldn't it be better to pray more specifically? "God, I ask that you bless Brother John with good health. Give him favor on his job. Provide for the financial needs of his family . . ." Get the idea? Generic prayers produce generic results. Be specific.

8. **Vary your prayer activities.** Pray with a list. When someone asks you to pray, write it down. A list will help you pray for the things you might otherwise forget.

9. **Pray and meditate on Scripture.** The Bible is filled with promises of God. Spend part of your prayer time reading and meditating on some of them. Ask God how you should apply these promises to your personal life. Pray the promises for others. I have unsaved family members for whom I

often claim the promises of God, believing they will one day know God.

10. **Take time to listen.** God speaks in that still small voice. Quiet your spirit and listen to what He has to say to you.

11. **Ask God to direct your prayer time.** I once heard a speaker who said he started his prayer time with a notepad and a pen. He would sit down and say, "Okay, God, what would You have me pray for today?" What a wonderful idea! If we are truly Spirit led, then our prayer time should be as well. Ask God what He wants you to pray for and then listen for His answer.

12. **Try different postures.** Spend part of your prayer time going through the different postures or positions of prayer: kneel, stand, prostrate, bow, lift hands, sit, and walk.

13. **Pray with an agenda.** Have a different prayer focus each day of the week. On Monday, pray for government leaders. On Tuesday, family and friends. On Wednesday, worldwide revival. On Thursday, pray through your local newspaper. You get the idea.

14. **Multitask prayer with low concentration jobs.** Take advantage of the time spent doing things that don't require a lot of concentration. Pray while you are driving to

work (but please keep your eyes open!). Pray while vacuuming. Pray while cutting the grass. Pray while jogging in the morning or evening. And while you pray, why not pray for your neighborhood?

15. **Keep a prayer journal.** When God answers a prayer, write it down. What better way to build your faith than to look back on all the times God has answered your prayers in the past. The list could also be used for a time of praise and thanksgiving. As you get older, you tend to forget. Write it down and let it be a testimony of God's power. Remember, He is the same yesterday, today, and forever. If He did it then, He can do it again.

16. **Pray for yourself and for others.** The old adage says it well: "They need the prayer and you need the practice."

17. **Have a prayer partner.** Having a prayer partner not only multiplies your power (one can put 1,000 to flight, two can rout 10,000) but it also provides accountability. It can build unity and close friendships. Often we unwisely try to fight battles alone. Prayer partners provide support during difficult times and remind us that God intended for us to bear one another's burdens.

To enlarge your understanding of prayer, read books on prayer and study prayer in the Word of God. The more you pray, the more you will want to pray. When you see the positive impact it has on your life, you will be hooked.

PRAYING THE WORD

Prayer is not for the purpose of getting everything we want from God. Prayer is the way *God gets His will done on this earth.* Our all-powerful God has chosen, to a large extent, to limit His power to the prayers of His people.

How do we know what God's will is? We can be completely confident that God's will is contained in the pages of His Word. Praying the Word of God is praying powerfully and totally in the will of God. It is almost as if we can step into God's mind or His thoughts and pray according to His will, knowing He will hear us.

> *"And we can be confident that He will listen to us whenever we ask Him for anything in line with His will. And if we know He is listening when we make our requests, we can be sure He will give us what we ask for"* (I John 5:14, 15, NLT).

The most powerful thing a Christian can do is pray the Word of God. The Word is quick and powerful. We know when we pray the Word, it reaches the throne of God and shakes the foundation of the enemy.

God's Word is essential to your prayer life. It is the fuel behind every effective prayer. Jesus left no room for doubt about that. In the Gospel of John, He forever linked the Word with answered prayer by saying, *"If ye abide in me, and my words abide in you, ye shall ask what ye will, and it shall be done unto you"* (John 15:7).

When your Word level gets low, you'll find your prayers sputtering and lurching along instead of roaring ahead in power. If you don't stop and refuel, your praying will eventually come to a complete stop. Praying the Word is not just nice-sounding phrases; it is the very substance of God Himself. You see, the words of God "are spirit, and they are life" (John 6:63). They do for your inner man what food does for your outer man. Just as the food you eat supplies energy to your physical body, when you digest the Word of God it supplies your prayers with energy.

When you pray the Word, you are praying God Himself right into the middle of your situation.

Here are a few examples to get you started.

Insecure? *"I will never leave you nor forsake you"* *(Hebrews 13:5).* God, I am thankful that no matter what happens in life, I know you will never leave me nor forsake me.

Need salvation? *"If we confess our sins, He is faithful and just to forgive us our sins and to cleanse us from all unrighteousness" (I John 1:9).* God, I am so thankful I can come to you in repentance and you are faithful and just to forgive me and cleanse me from unrighteousness.

Going through a difficult time? *"God is our refuge and strength, a very present help in trouble" (Psalm 46:1).* God, your word tells me that you are my refuge and strength. I am in trouble and I need your help.

Life's troubles have you down? *"Weeping may endure for a night, but joy comes in the morning" (Psalm 30:5).* Lord Jesus, I know Your word says that weeping may endure for the night, but joy comes in the morning. I am believing this trial will pass and joy will once again be restored to my life.

Need provision? *"And my God shall supply all your need according to His riches in glory by Christ Jesus" (Philippians 4:19).* God, your word tells me that you will supply all of my needs according to Your riches. I ask for the need I have to be supplied today.

Need healing? *"Is anyone among you sick? Let him call for the elders of the church, and let them pray over him, anointing him with oil in the name of the Lord. And the prayer of faith will save the sick, and the Lord will raise him up. And if he has committed sins, he will be forgiven" (James 5:14-15).* According to Your word, I claim my healing and repent knowing you will forgive my sins.

Struggling with fear? *"For God has not given us a*

spirit of fear, but of power, and of love and of a sound mind" *(II Timothy 1:7).* Lord, I come against fear because it is not from You.

Lacking peace? *"And the peace of God, which surpasses all understanding, will guard your hearts and minds through Christ Jesus" (Philippians 4:7).* Lord, I need your peace that passes understanding in my life and in my circumstance.

Hurting? *"He heals the brokenhearted and binds up their wounds" (Psalm 147:3).* Jesus, I am hurting and Your word says you will heal the brokenhearted and bind their wounds. I need that today and I believe You will do it for me.

Need strength? *"But those who wait on the Lord shall renew their strength; they shall mount up with wings like eagles, they shall run and not be weary, they shall walk and not faint" (Isaiah 40:31).* Lord, I feel as thought I can't go on. I have waited patiently on your God and I am standing on Your word that You will renew my strength.

Need confidence? *"I can do all things through Christ who strengthens me" (Philippians 4:13).* Lord Jesus, I feel very inadequate, but Your word tells me that I can do all things through You, so I am stepping out in faith knowing that You will empower me to do the task at hand.

Struggling with your past? *"Therefore, if anyone is in Christ, he is a new creation; old things have passed away; behold, all things have become new" (II Corinthians 5:17).*

God, according to Your word, I am a new creation. My past mistakes are gone. Help me see my value as You do.

Need assurance? *"Now to Him who is able to do exceedingly abundantly above all that we ask or think, according to the power that works in us"* (Ephesians 3:20). Jesus, my situation is big, but my God is bigger. You are able to do exceedingly, abundantly, above all I can ask or think.

Need self-confidence? *"If God is for us, who can be against us?"* (Romans 8:31). Lord, it feels as though all of hell is coming at me. But Your word tells me that if You are for me, who is against me doesn't even matter. I rejoice because you are on my side.

ABOUT THE AUTHOR

Lisa Marshall is the Strategic Prayer Coordinator for the World Network of Prayer and has traveled extensively, teaching and speaking on the subject of prayer.

Made in the USA
Middletown, DE
16 March 2022